TIPS FOR SUCCESS™

TOP 10 TIPS FOR PLANNING FOR A CAREER

MOLLY JONES

ROSEN
PUBLISHING®

NEW YORK

Published in 2013 by The Rosen Publishing Group, Inc.
29 East 21st Street, New York, NY 10010

First Edition

Library of Congress Cataloging-in-Publication Data

Jones, Molly, 1933–
Top 10 tips for planning for a career/Molly Jones. — 1st ed.
p. cm. — (Tips for success)
Includes bibliographical references and index.
ISBN 978-1-4488-6863-6 (library binding)
1. Vocational guidance—Juvenile literature. 2. Occupations—Juvenile literature.
I. Title. II. Title: Top ten tips for planning for a career.
HF5381.2.J66 2012
650.1–dc23

                                                                        2012006834

Manufactured in the United States of America

CPSIA Compliance Information: Batch #S12YA: For further information, contact Rosen Publishing, New York, New York, at 1-800-237-9932.

CONTENTS

INTRODUCTION

What will you do with your abilities, your values, and the opportunities that will come to you over your lifetime? Your career will be the answer. Your career will be the lifelong contribution you make to your family, your community, and your world in return for the contributions others make that benefit you.

At one time, a young adult might have expected to work for all of his or her life in the same job. Some worked in a family business or on a family farm. Others studied for and practiced a profession such as accounting, dentistry, or teaching. Some devoted their lives to scientific research, manufacturing, or technology, and they used those skills in the same job until retirement.

Today, however, few young adults will hold the same type of job for a lifetime. The pervasiveness and acceleration of change

Knock your career out of the ballpark

A student explores careers at a job fair in Oklahoma City, Oklahoma. A winning career is one that matches your abilities and interests with an important local or global need.

in today's world demand a new kind of career preparation. Young adults today not only need basic skills and knowledge, but also the ability to apply them to a wide range of occupations. They need to be flexible in their thinking, open to new ideas, and willing to master new ways of doing things. Although some workers may still stay in the same job for decades, the U.S. Department of Labor predicts that most young adults today will change jobs or even professions several times in their working lives.

Now is not the time to make a final decision about a career but to begin your career planning. A good career plan is one you choose after much research into the world of work. You'll also want to explore your personal characteristics and how they fit into that world. Society's many needs require many kinds of work. People are needed to do manual, technical, scientific, creative, and managerial work; all of these areas of skill are responsible for valuable contributions. Beginning now allows time to consider what you value most in life, to observe many lifestyles and types of work, to explore the world's needs and problems, and to discover ways you can be part of their solutions. Then you can follow the learning path that will help you fulfill your goals.

You might not have realized that, while still a student, you can actually become part of the world of work and begin gaining useful knowledge and experience. Within your school and community you can discover, or create for yourself, opportunities to "try on" many careers via research, observation, volunteering, job shadowing, and participating in activities. You can have fun while acquiring some expertise.

The ten tips offered in the chapters ahead will help you begin finding your own path toward a fulfilling career. The first important step is to get to know yourself.

KNOW YOURSELF

Though it may now seem distant, the time will come when you are finished with school and are ready to enter the career world. Once in a full-time job, you may spend one-third or more of your life at work. With that much of your life invested in work, it's important to plan a career where you can use your abilities to their fullest extent and pursue objectives that are consistent with your values. You also want to choose a career in which your personality type will be an asset. To begin planning, learn all you can about your working preferences and your personality traits.

UNCOVERING THE REAL YOU

Four questions will help you uncover your unique combination of traits and begin planning for your life at work:

> 1. What are your interests—the things you most like to do and care most about?

T. C. Williams High School in Alexandria, Virginia, provides students with course options that can lead to career opportunities. These students are learning food preparation skills.

2. What are your top talents—the kinds of things you do best?

3. What is your real potential—the level at which you could achieve and contribute if you were motivated to do your absolute best?

4. What are your values—the things you believe are most important in life?

To find the best career fit, you'll also want to discover how you work and think best and examine how you relate to and interact with others.

DISCOVERING YOUR DEEPEST INTERESTS

You may think you know quite well what your interests are. In time, though, you may realize that you do many things because your friends are doing them or because your parents or teachers expect you to do them, when you may prefer to do something very different. Your choice of a career may be influenced in the same way. How can you separate your own interests from the interests and expectations of others?

Begin by making a list of several major ways you've spent time in the past, such as taking piano lessons, playing in a soccer league, spending summers at camp, reading mystery novels, or hiking with friends. Which ones did you choose because you really wanted to do them? Which were you required or persuaded to do? Which did you dread, and which did you wish you could do more of?

Also, ask yourself some questions. If you could choose any career in the world, would you choose a job in which you work alone or work with others? Outdoors or indoors? If you could

YOUR PERSONALITY AND YOUR CAREER

Psychologist John L. Holland defined six personality types and the kinds of work environments in which each would fit best.

Personality Type	Preferred Work Environment
Realistic	Practical, physical, hands-on
Investigative	Analytical, intellectual, scientific, exploratory
Artistic	Creative, original, independent, chaotic
Social	Cooperative, supporting, helping, healing, nurturing
Enterprising	Competitive, leading, persuading
Conventional	Detail-oriented, organizing, clerical

Holland's description of personality types can be found in his book *Making Vocational Choices: A Theory of Vocational Personalities and Work Environments.*

choose any books in the library for your school reading, what subjects would you choose to read about?

After thinking about your true preferences, ask your teacher or guidance counselor about taking an interest inventory or preference test. These tests are designed to give you an objective view of what your real interests are and offer evidence of what kinds of work you would find most rewarding.

UNDERSTANDING YOUR APTITUDES

Your aptitudes, or talents, are often suggested by your favorite activities or subjects, the ones in which you feel most competent and do your best work. What achievements are you most proud of? In what subjects do you make your best grades?

Through science fairs, students develop research and presentation skills essential for science careers. In St. Augustine, Florida, Alex Lowe and Reana Greene explain how they detected elevated pesticide levels at a nearby elementary school.

However, many people have an aptitude for a type of activity or work they are not aware of and haven't had an opportunity to experience. Your teacher or guidance counselor can administer an aptitude test to help you identify those areas in which you have the greatest ability. This insight can guide you toward investigating careers in which you would be most likely to succeed.

WHAT DO YOU VALUE MOST?

Your values, that is, the things you believe to be most important in life, guide the choices you make. Will it be more important to you to earn a high salary, receive personal recognition, or realize that you have made other people's lives better?

Analyze the reasons for the choices you've made in the past. What have been the most important factors in your decisions, and what outcomes have given you the most satisfaction? Recognizing your values can help you choose a career that supports those values.

WHAT IS YOUR PERSONALITY TYPE?

Your personality traits are often revealed in the ways you interact with others. Are you shy or outgoing? Do you prefer working alone or as part of a team? Are your decisions based more on your feelings about a situation or by gathering factual information and thinking about it? Are you more competitive or more cooperative? Personality inventories can help you identify and understand your traits. These, too, may be available through your guidance counselor.

Any career area is likely to include a range of jobs suitable for different personality types. Keep your personality traits, values, interests, and aptitudes in mind as you explore the world of careers.

EXPLORE A WIDE RANGE OF CAREERS

Beginning to explore your career options now gives you the time and opportunity to investigate a wide range of careers, including areas you formerly knew little about or had little interest in.

According to career counselors Susan Maltz and Barbara Grahn, most young adults explore far fewer career areas and job possibilities than might be suitable to them. While still a student, you can observe people who work in a variety of areas and consider how your abilities and interests would fit with similar jobs.

COMPUTERS AND CAREERS: WHAT WILL COMPUTERS DO TOMORROW?

Dr. Eberhard Fetz, professor of physiology and biophysics at the University of Washington, has been doing groundbreaking work with his research team. In laboratory experiments with monkeys, they enabled a computer to restore the brain's control of bodily movements after nerve connections were temporarily blocked with anesthetics. Their goal is to apply this capability to humans who have lost various physical abilities.

In physics, scientists at the Institute of Nanotechnology say that tomorrow's new technology will dramatically increase computer processing speed, as well as the capacity to transfer and store information in smaller and smaller spaces.

In many of tomorrow's careers, computers will play an important role. Thinking ahead about your career will allow you time to build strong computer skills and knowledge.

DISCOVERING WHERE YOU FIT IN

One way to describe careers is by the type and purpose of their activities. For example, careers in health and medicine, finance and banking, environmental management, the arts, food preparation and service, or agriculture represent many types of work and a wide range of objectives. Books in your public or school library about careers can help you consider whether the values represented by each career field are compatible with your own goals and ideals.

High school sophomores and juniors in Sacramento, California, take advantage of career counseling offered by adult volunteers.

As you read about each field that interests you, notice the range of job possibilities in that field. For example, organizations that focus on environmental issues may need financial workers to manage budgets and accounting, office workers to do clerical and administrative tasks, computer analysts to manage data and records, engineers to design and supervise major projects, biochemists to design experiments and analyze samples, wildlife biologists and field workers to do animal and plant studies, and more.

Once you've discovered one or more career areas and jobs within them that match your interests and aptitudes, begin to research the education and training that each requires. Insert a career field that interests you into your computer browser. You might enter such phrases as "environmental careers," "medical careers," "writing careers," or "auto repair careers," and choose links related to education and training for that field. Typical salaries in the field can also be explored.

In addition to your browser, books such as *Best Career and Education Web Sites: A Quick Guide to Online Job Search* by Anne Wolfinger can help you locate career information quickly on the Web. Also, you can find information about careers by browsing business and professional magazines in your public library. In upcoming tips, you'll discover the many ways that you can observe and experience work in your areas of interest while still a student.

STUDY THE CHANGING CAREER OUTLOOK

As you explore career possibilities, it's a good idea to learn about job prospects in your community, as well as nationally and globally. No matter how interesting a career might seem, no one wants to invest time and money in studying, planning, and training for a career and then find no jobs available in that field after graduating from school or college.

Just as other factors in our lives change, the career world, too, changes constantly. Unneeded jobs disappear, and new needs spur the creation of new jobs. Also, job possibilities may increase in one community yet decrease in another when businesses or manufacturing plants build new facilities and close old ones. Today, accelerating change in almost every area of life makes it critical to stay well aware of the job outlook.

HOW DO LIFESTYLE AND ECONOMIC CHANGES AFFECT CAREER PROSPECTS?

Changes in lifestyles, the environment, national and world economies, and technology all affect job prospects. As people change their daily patterns of living, fewer workers are needed in jobs

Kingston High School students in West Park, New York, observe some of the skills and knowledge that environmental scientist Chris Bowser employs in his career. Here, Bowser checks his net for American eels.

17

that support outdated ways. New jobs are being created to support new ways of living.

In farming and the growing of livestock, new technology has brought about enormous changes. Large-scale agricultural careers, in which many farm tasks are automated, require different skills from those needed on smaller family- or community-operated farms. In the past, foods produced on small family farms were largely consumed locally, within the community or state where they were produced. Much of today's mass-produced food is consumed great distances away, often in other parts of the world. Other changes that affect agricultural careers include:

- The accelerating growth of the world's population
- Urbanization, that is, the tendency of the population to shift toward urban areas and away from rural areas
- The increasing demand for organically grown food
- The growing interest in agroecology, that is, the development of farming procedures that protect the environment while meeting the world's growing food requirements

Science and technology are expanding our understanding of the environment. As a result, many new careers are appearing in environmental science, technology, and fieldwork related to protecting and managing the environment.

National and world economics, as well as local government decisions about taxes, job creation, and other issues, affect job availability. While economic conditions are often temporary, any period of job uncertainty underscores the importance of being competent in skills and knowledge that are useful in more than one job.

In government and private industry, advancing computer technology means more jobs are done by computers and fewer are done by people. For example, as businesses and individuals print more of

WHERE WILL THE JOBS BE?

Below are occupations projected to show the largest percentage of growth by 2018, according to the U.S. Department of Labor and the U.S. Bureau of Labor Statistics.

Occupation	Projected Percent Growth by 2018
Biomedical engineers	72%
Network systems and data communications analysts	53%
Home health aides	50%
Personal and home care aides	46%
Financial examiners	41%
Medical scientists (except epidemiologists)	40%
Physician assistants	39%
Skin-care specialists	38%
Biochemists and biophysicists	37%
Athletic trainers	37%

Additional careers projected to grow rapidly in the near future can be found in the *Occupational Outlook Handbook* and other government publications in your public library.

their own books and documents using computers and printers, printing companies hire fewer workers, and some even go out of business. Similarly, as more books are downloaded to electronic reading devices, publishing companies may print fewer books and hire fewer workers.

However, in spite of the changes in the number and types of jobs, the skills of reading, writing, mathematics, critical thinking, and problem solving will remain essential. In an article in the *New York Times*, Steve Lohr noted that human traits such as creativity and intuition will always be needed in the workplace.

STAYING ON TOP OF CHANGE

How has the career outlook changed in your community? Your local chamber of commerce, an organization that represents businesses in the area, can provide you with information about local businesses. The U.S. Department of Labor publishes new information every other year about the nation's job outlook in hundreds of fields. Its *Occupational Outlook Handbook* is available in most public libraries and on the Web at http://www.bls.gov/oco. In it you can learn not only what careers are "growing" or "shrinking," but also the typical salaries each job might offer. Another important benefit of examining the *Occupational Outlook Handbook* is discovering job possibilities you've never considered and may want to explore.

MASTER THE BASICS

Many skill and knowledge areas that have always been basic to work success are still important in career preparation. Among these are mathematics and language, including reading, writing, and communication skills. However, rapid change in the world of careers has expanded the list of basics that are essential to job success in the twenty-first century. In addition to new basic skills and knowledge, careers today and in the future will require new ways of thinking and working.

ESSENTIAL SKILLS FOR A CHANGING CAREER WORLD

While they are not new, the following areas of skill are increasingly important for those seeking well-paying, rewarding careers.

A student demonstrates her understanding of a math problem. Along with competence in language, science, and computer skills, mastery of basic math has become essential in career preparation.

Mathematics. In this age of technology and automation, being competent in basic math skills is essential in almost every job and daily activity. Math skills and understanding are needed in computer and technological applications and development, as well as in the fields of science, business, and engineering.

Language: Reading, Writing, and Communicating. Developing the habit of reading and writing daily, and working to excel in both, will help you in every subject you study and in any career you pursue. Mastering language skills will be the key to understanding and learning, whether from books or electronic sources, and to communicating your knowledge and views to others.

Science. While basic scientific knowledge and an understanding of the scientific method have long been important, these concepts have now become indispensable in today's career world, and their importance will grow in the future. Scientific research is the foundation of advances in technology, health, and many other areas.

THINK COMPUTERS

The Association for Computing Machinery (ACM), an organization for computing professionals, encourages all students to include computer study in their career preparation, whatever area they plan to enter. Its Computing Careers Web site for young people (http://computingcareers.acm.org) states:

> Computing and computer technology are part of just about everything that touches our lives from the cars we drive, to the movies we watch, to the way businesses and governments deal with us. Understanding different dimensions of computing is part of the necessary skill set for an educated person in the 21st century. Whether you want to be a scientist, develop the latest killer application, or just know what it really means when someone says "the computer made a mistake," studying computing will provide you with valuable knowledge.

Computer and Communications Technology. According to the Association for Computing Machinery, computing jobs are among the highest paid and have the highest job satisfaction. In other careers, too, strong computer skills are essential for locating needed information, organizing it in a useful way, and communicating it efficiently to others.

ESSENTIAL WAYS OF THINKING AND WORKING

Rapid change in every area of life requires workers to be able to shift their talents and knowledge to new projects and focus on meeting new goals. Also, as technology replaces people in many jobs, the human ability to apply higher-level thinking processes to workplace needs will become increasingly important. The essential thinking and working skills include:

- **Adaptability.** With this skill, one can apply experience and knowledge gained in one area to learning new skills and becoming competent in other areas.
- **Critical thinking.** One can analyze a situation and correctly identify problems.
- **Creative thinking and inventiveness.** One can conceive of and implement new approaches to solving problems and challenges.

Becoming competent both in basic and higher-level skills will boost your prospects in a wide range of interesting careers.

MYTHS & FACTS

MYTH: TO BE WELL PREPARED FOR CAREERS, STUDENTS NO LONGER NEED TO LEARN MATHEMATICS SKILLS AND FACTS BECAUSE COMPUTERS CAN NOW PROVIDE ANSWERS INSTANTLY.

FACT: COMPUTERS CAN PROVIDE INSTANT WRONG ANSWERS AS EASILY AS INSTANT RIGHT ONES IF THE INFORMATION ENTERED IS

INCORRECT. KNOWING AND UNDERSTANDING MATHEMATICAL FACTS AND RELATIONSHIPS ARE NECESSARY FOR THE USER TO APPLY THE CORRECT PROCEDURE AND ESTIMATE THE CORRECT ANSWER AS A CHECK ON THE PROCESS.

MYTH: A COLLEGE DEGREE IS BECOMING LESS IMPORTANT IN THE WORKPLACE.

FACT: ACCORDING TO AN ARTICLE IN *U.S. NEWS & WORLD REPORT*, MARTHA J. KANTER, UNDERSECRETARY FOR THE U.S. DEPARTMENT OF EDUCATION, HAS STATED THAT THE COUNTRY MUST PRODUCE MORE COLLEGE GRADUATES IN ORDER TO FILL THE HIGH-SKILLED JOBS THAT WILL ADVANCE THE ECONOMY. ALSO, STUDY RESULTS RELEASED BY GEORGETOWN UNIVERSITY'S CENTER ON EDUCATION AND THE WORKFORCE REVEALED THAT THE LIFETIME EARNINGS OF COLLEGE GRADUATES ARE 84 PERCENT HIGHER THAN THE EARNINGS OF HIGH SCHOOL GRADUATES.

MYTH: THE MAIN EFFECT OF GLOBALIZATION IS THAT WORKERS IN OTHER COUNTRIES ARE TAKING AWAY AMERICAN JOBS.

FACT: WHILE GLOBALIZATION HAS RESULTED IN SOME AMERICAN JOBS MOVING OVERSEAS, THERE ARE ALSO POSITIVE EFFECTS. GLOBALIZATION IS ENABLING THE BEST MINDS FROM AROUND THE WORLD TO WORK TOGETHER ON PROBLEMS THAT AFFECT EVERYONE, SUCH AS POVERTY, MAJOR DISEASES, AND ENVIRONMENTAL ISSUES SUCH AS GLOBAL WARMING.

JOIN THE CAREER WORLD NOW

Having explored a range of career possibilities, as well as your strongest aptitudes and interests, you can now move out into the career world. Take advantage of any opportunities to observe and experience what careers in your fields of interest would actually be like.

COMPARING THE DREAM TO THE REALITY

A good test of your dream career comes when you discover first-hand what people in that field actually do each day. What are the ways you can observe and experience what a job in your field of interest would be like?

PRACTICING PROFESSIONAL COURTESY

Developing good habits in your interactions with others will help prepare you for successful interviews when you begin seeking a full-time job. Examples of professional courtesy include:

- Dressing appropriately. Dress codes differ in different offices, but grooming and cleanliness are always essential.
- Listening to others. Listening well is sometimes difficult. Practice active listening by making eye contact and focusing your attention on the other person, working to understand what he or she wants to communicate.
- Speaking respectfully and appropriately to everyone, whether in person or through written messages.
- Expressing appreciation for a person's assistance, time, and work.
- Being on time. This is an essential way of showing respect to others.

Courtesy means showing consideration for the feelings and needs of others. Whether working in your career or planning for your career, showing courtesy toward everyone will prove to be a valuable habit.

JOB SHADOWING AND INTERVIEWING

Job shadowing means visiting a person who works in a career field you'd like to know about, accompanying him or her through the working day, and observing what his or her workday is really like. Some schools arrange job-shadowing opportunities for their

Montana high school student Shawna Cary shadows photographer Steve Helmbrecht for an in-depth look at a career in photography. Helmbrecht explains lighting techniques used in portrait photography.

students in cooperation with businesses in the community. If your school does not have a job-shadowing program, arrange your own opportunity through neighbors or friends.

When you shadow or interview a person, find out all you can about the business or organization before going and plan your questions in advance. Your preparation will show your host that you appreciate his or her time, and it will ensure that you obtain as much useful information as possible.

CONNECTING WITH A MENTOR

A mentor is an adult whom you admire and trust and who can offer guidance in important decisions about school, your personal life, and your career. A mentor can also help you set up opportu-

nities such as job shadowing, interviewing, or doing part-time or volunteer work in a field of interest. According to career counselors Maltz and Grahn, studies have shown a direct link between having a mentor and success in school and work.

VOLUNTEERING OR WORKING PART-TIME

The benefits of volunteering and summer or part-time work are important. Even when unpaid, working in a field you

In Redding, California, high school student Betty Kerby serves her community by volunteering at an animal shelter. At the same time, she gains valuable career experience in animal care.

are considering as a career provides the opportunity to experience what the job is like from the inside. In fact, all kinds of work experiences can give you confidence and competence, whether or not they are in your field of interest.

10 GREAT QUESTIONS
TO ASK A GUIDANCE COUNSELOR

1 DOES OUR SCHOOL HAVE AN ORGANIZED JOB-SHADOWING PROGRAM WITH LOCAL BUSINESSES?

2 HOW CAN I ARRANGE TO TAKE AN APTITUDE TEST TO DISCOVER MY STRONGEST ABILITIES?

3 HOW CAN I ARRANGE TO TAKE A PREFERENCE TEST TO DISCOVER MY REAL INTERESTS?

4 WHAT CAREERS ARE SUGGESTED BY MY GRADES AND PERSONAL CHARACTERISTICS?

5 WHERE CAN I FIND A PART-TIME JOB RELATED TO MY CAREER INTERESTS?

6 HOW CAN I FIND A MENTOR IN MY COMMUNITY?

7 DO YOU KNOW ABOUT A CAREER DAY AT WHICH MEMBERS OF COMMUNITY BUSINESSES AND ORGANIZATIONS TALK TO STUDENTS ABOUT CAREERS? CAN OUR SCHOOL SPONSOR ONE?

8 WHICH COLLEGES HAVE THE BEST PROGRAMS IN THE CAREER FIELD I'M INTERESTED IN?

9 ARE THERE BUSINESSES IN MY COMMUNITY THAT OFFER INTERNSHIPS FOR STUDENTS WHO WOULD LIKE TO GET WORK EXPERIENCE?

10 WHAT ELECTIVE COURSES WOULD SUPPORT MY MAIN CAREER INTEREST?

TIP #6

INVESTIGATE THE WORLD OF SELF-EMPLOYMENT

eople who work for themselves, owning and operating their own businesses, are called entrepreneurs. Many successful, well-known people have been entrepreneurs. In 1903, after working as an engineer in Thomas Edison's Illuminating Company in Detroit, Henry Ford founded the Ford Motor Company. While he employed many other people, he was an entrepreneur, working for himself in his own business.

More than a century later, following many other successful entrepreneurs, Steve Jobs became well known as cofounder of Apple Computer. *Inc.* magazine named Jobs "Entrepreneur of

The Opportunity Fund, a nonprofit lender, helped entrepreneur Manuel Godino open his own empanada shop in San Francisco, California.

the Decade." Though the names of Jobs and Ford are known around the world, not all entrepreneurs are successful.

Professionals in many types of work can be either self-employed or hired to work in someone else's business. For example, while some farmers are employed by other farmers or by agricultural corporations, many own their own land and work for themselves. An accountant may work in his or her own office or work in another business or corporation.

Some students planning for a career may find self-employment to be an attractive option for developing the kind of career they

TRAITS OF SUCCESSFUL ENTREPRENEURS

Some people seem to prefer self-employment, and others prefer working for someone else. According to an article on BusinessInsider.com, the Guardian Life Small Business Research Institute investigated the personality traits of successful self-employed people. The research found that the following six traits seemed to characterize the most successful entrepreneurs:

- Ability to work well with others, delegate tasks to others, and motivate others successfully
- Curiosity and persistence in searching for ways to improve the business
- Tendency to stay focused on trends and future developments that might affect the business
- Valuing the freedom to make their own choices more than the security of a corporate position
- Staying informed and up-to-date on technology
- Being inspired to work harder when difficulties arise, rather than being discouraged

Comparing your own preferences and personal traits to those discovered in the research may help you determine whether your style of working might fit the profile of a successful entrepreneur.

envision. Self-employment presents special challenges as well as special rewards. Understanding these challenges and rewards can help you decide if the world of self-employment would be right for you or if you would be happier working for someone else.

CHALLENGES OF SELF-EMPLOYMENT

In addition to practicing their own professions, entrepreneurs must handle business tasks that, if they worked for someone else, would be done by others. One such task is to constantly advertise or publicize their business to keep work coming in.

Self-employment offers both rewards and challenges. Managing finances, taxes, personnel, supplies, and equipment can all be part of this business owner's responsibilities.

Another task is to keep records of all business transactions and work. Financial records of income and expenses must be maintained. Taxes must be calculated and paid. Employees must be paid, and the workplace structure must be maintained. Entrepreneurs must seek, hire, train, and supervise any needed employees.

Those who own their own businesses bear the risk of losing money if their businesses don't succeed. Their income may be unpredictable, depending on how much work they have. They must provide any benefits they and their employees will have, such as health insurance.

Self-employed people often work long hours to complete their work and take care of all business responsibilities. They are responsible for the quality of work the business does and for having the knowledge, experience, and skills that their business requires.

BENEFITS OF SELF-EMPLOYMENT

In spite of the challenges of self-employment, millions of people choose to work for themselves, rather than for someone else. According to *USA TODAY*, 14.5 million people were self-employed in September 2011. For the happily self-employed, the benefits outweigh the challenges. What benefits do entrepreneurs find in working for themselves?

Self-employed workers can make their own rules, follow their own interests, and set their own hours. They are free to experiment and try out their ideas. Not having to answer to anyone else, they can set the pace of their work, taking on as much or as little as they choose. They profit from their own efforts, rather than having their efforts benefit someone else.

Should you consider being an entrepreneur? Thinking about both the benefits and the challenges of self-employment can help you decide whether it might be an option for your future.

SHARPEN YOUR SUCCESS SKILLS

Everyone has his or her own idea of success. A person's values, objectives, and beliefs about his or her strengths and limitations work together to shape what he or she would consider success. To one young person, success may mean landing the role of a young piano artist with the regional orchestra. To another, success may mean making it down the steps alone for the first time with new leg braces. The first young person feels successful because he is moving toward his goal of winning a piano scholarship at the Julliard School of Music. The second feels successful because she is moving toward her goal of being able to live independently. Though their goals are different, both are moving toward the objectives they have set for themselves.

WHAT DO SUCCESSFUL PEOPLE SAY ABOUT SUCCESS?

The views of people who described success in the past differ very little from the views of those who discuss the topic today.

Nothing can stop the man with the right mental attitude from achieving his goal; nothing on earth can help the man with the wrong mental attitude. —Thomas Jefferson

To climb steep hills requires a slow pace at first. —William Shakespeare

Try not to become a person of success but a person of value. —Albert Einstein

Success is the sum of small efforts, repeated day in and day out. —Robert Collier

Let me tell you the secret that has led me to my goal. My strength lies solely in my tenacity. —Louis Pasteur

Whether scientists, writers, or statesmen, these famous leaders have attributed their success not to wealth or high intellect, but to persistence and character, traits that everyone can develop and apply.

PLANNING FOR A SUCCESSFUL CAREER

The paths to success in academics, work, relationships, and life in general will differ in some ways. However, many experts point to several common principles that will increase your chances for success in any venture, including your career.

1. Set goals and objectives. Success is seeing yourself take one small step at a time toward your goals.

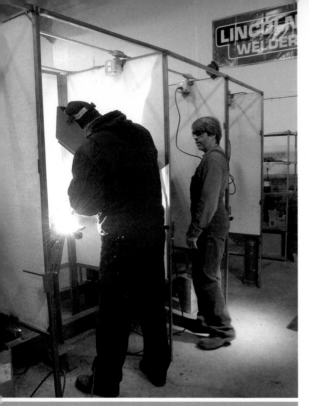

Experienced welder James Stanton operates a mentoring program in Oregon. Here, he observes as a mentee practices a welding technique.

For example, in your career notebook, write each long-term goal you'd like to reach. Leave room underneath and write in the steps you need to take as you work them out.

2. Take responsibility for yourself, your actions, and your choices. Don't blame other people or outside forces for where you are in life. Recognize that, in large part, your choices have determined where you are now, and they will determine your future. Learn from choices that haven't turned out well, and put what you learn into action.

3. Practice a "win-win" approach to working with others. Stephen Covey, author of *The 7 Habits of Highly Effective People*, says that career success is influenced by how well one can work with others in many situations. Helping other people succeed as you work toward your own success will build strong relationships.

4. Be proactive. Don't wait for others to create opportunities for you. Take the initiative to find and create opportunities for yourself. For example, seek a mentor on your own if your school doesn't provide a mentoring program. If your school doesn't offer a job-shadowing program, call or visit a workplace of interest to arrange to interview or shadow a staff person, or ask an adult to help you arrange this. Ask an appropriate person for information or help whenever you need it.

5. Practice self-determination. Choose your own life direction based on the person you are, what you do best, and your own values. Don't follow the lead of others whose values and objectives are different from yours.

6. Practice perseverance. Jack Canfield, author of *The Success Principles: How to Get from Where You Are to Where You Want to Be*, believes that persistence is the quality most often found in high achievers. To succeed in reaching your career goals, refuse to give up when things get tough. The successful person is seldom the luckiest or the smartest person, but the one who learns from mistakes and keeps working toward his or her objectives.

Planning and preparing for a career is a long process, not a single event. Keeping the principles of success in mind at each decision point, plan to move toward your goals, taking one step at a time.

POLISH YOUR SELF-PRESENTATION

The time will soon come when you need to present yourself in a strong, positive, and confident way as a great potential employee. Creating and taking advantage of practice opportunities will build confidence and skills, first to seek and land the job of your choice, and then to perform well as a new worker.

BUILD CONFIDENCE WITH PREPARATION AND PRACTICE

Everyone has strengths and weaknesses in how they interact with others, but often people are unaware of their weaker traits. Unfortunately, negative habits can prevent people from making the impression they'd hoped to make in their interview, presentation, or group project. Discovering ways to improve your self-presentation now will give you time and opportunities to change weaknesses into assets.

Attending job fairs and career days can offer insights into a wide range of career possibilities while allowing you to practice your self-presentation.

While engaging in career planning, you will have many chances to practice self-presentation. Examples include shadowing someone in an interesting career, talking to a staff person about a part-time job, presenting a research report to your class, and asking someone to become your mentor. All of these are good opportunities to perfect your presentation skills and prepare for future interviews.

Every interview or meeting has two important parts: your preparation and your performance. How well prepared you are will determine your success during the meeting or interview.

BE PREPARED

Before an interview, find out anything you can about the person with whom you will be talking, such as the person's job title and work responsibilities. If your intent is to job-shadow, interview employees for information, or apply for a part-time or volunteer job, also research the business or organization. Often an office or organization has a Web site with information about the business and staff. Being informed in advance will help you ask intelligent questions and show genuine interest in the work.

Think ahead about what questions you may be asked and how you will answer them. Practice your answers. Also plan what

PRESENT YOURSELF IN WRITING: BUILD YOUR RÉSUMÉ NOW

What is a résumé? A résumé is a written summary of your education, work experience, and other experiences that make you qualified for a job, college, or other program. Your résumé can include a list or description of your skills for the job and whether or not you have used those skills in a previous job. You can find a sample résumé format in Microsoft Word.

What is the purpose of a résumé? A résumé is a written document to introduce yourself and your qualifications. When a business has a job opening, one or more staff persons read résumés of job applicants to decide whom they'd like to interview for the job. If you are invited in for an interview, the staff may ask questions about the information in your résumé and how your education and experience make you qualified for the job.

When should I write my résumé? Writing a practice résumé now will help you prepare for the time when you need your actual résumé. Although a résumé is a written document, you are building it every day. Your classes and grades, activities you participate in, offices you've held and responsibilities you've assumed, nonrequired courses you've taken, part-time or volunteer work you've done—all of these come together on your résumé to create a picture of the kind of person you are.

questions you want to ask and how you might follow up on the responses you get.

BE PROFESSIONAL

Show respect for the workplace and staff by arriving on time and being well groomed and appropriately dressed. Be pleasant but serious about the workplace and what you hope to accomplish. Show interest in the business and its objectives and in learning more about it.

Many employers now routinely research every applicant's "social" background as well as criminal background. Think carefully about any words or images you consider posting on social media or personal Web sites. Be sure your posts convey the image you would want a potential employer to see. Once you have posted material you could regret in the future, there may be no way to undo your carelessness.

EXPAND YOUR CAREER PERSPECTIVE: THINK GLOBALLY

Whether you study and work in the community where you were born or on the other side of the world, your life and career will be affected by globalization. Globalization—the tendency of nations, organizations, and individuals around the world to become increasingly more connected and interdependent—is not an entirely new process. In earlier centuries, the armies of the Roman Empire, the explorers of the Middle Ages, and the monarchs of the British Empire spread their languages and cultures to other parts of the world. What's new about globalization is the accelerating speed with which it is changing work and life. As a result, globalization is changing the way we think about and prepare for careers.

BE PREPARED: GLOBALIZATION AND YOUR CAREER

Whether your career keeps you close to home or sends you into the wider world, consider taking these steps toward becoming competent and confident in the global career environment:

- Widen your view of the kinds of careers you might consider. Be prepared by researching the global aspects of any career you investigate.
- Study at least one foreign language in high school and college. In your career preparation, consider careers in which a foreign language is needed.
- On your own or in courses you select, be a student of geography and the cultures of other countries.
- Join an international club to interact with students from other countries. If your school doesn't have one, suggest that one be organized.
- Suggest that your class invite a speaker from a local business that operates internationally. Ask how globalization affects his or her business and staff.

THINKING GLOBALLY

Thinking globally about careers means becoming aware of world needs, global ways of thinking, and worldwide opportunities. Global thinking also means being prepared to work effectively with people and ideas that may be unlike those you grew up with.

Globalization affects thinking and planning in business, economics, and manufacturing; health and medical care;

A giant globe in the Massachusetts State House focuses attention on Geography Education Week. Knowledge of geography and languages can open many career doors.

environmental protection and management; electronic information processing, communication, and media; food production, preparation, and distribution; conservation and allocation of natural resources and energy; human rights and needs; space exploration; and in many other areas. Decisions and actions taken in one country or community increasingly affect people in many other parts of the globe. Today, the issues and challenges in many fields reflect worldwide concerns.

YOUR GLOBALIZED LUNCH

Recently, the *Huffington Post* described how students at the California College of the Arts took a close look at globalization in everyday life. By investigating a single, relatively small aspect of their lives, the students discovered the amazing array of global resources that went into creating the taco they might buy at a nearby restaurant. From the corn in the taco shell to the tomatoes in the salsa, each student traced one ingredient back to its origin, noting every process the ingredient underwent to reach its final destination.

The investigation process wasn't easy. After spending hours on the phone interviewing many corporate customer representatives, the students produced a map that included farms, corporate offices, and the routes traveled by planes, trucks, and shipping containers. What did they find? The salt and the cheese were produced locally in California. However, the spices had traveled a combined distance of 15,000 miles (24,140 kilometers). The avocados had been grown in Chile, the rice in Thailand, and the tomatoes in the Southern Hemisphere. The aluminum in the foil wrapping was mined in New Zealand.

You can picture the jobs—not only on farms, but also in manufacturing, processing, packing, shipping, and finance—that were part of producing the taco. Related processes include development of international trade agreements and shipping regulations, Internet and wireless communications and transactions, and food quality inspections.

CAREERS WITHOUT BORDERS

Like careers in the food industry and almost every other area, environmental careers don't stop at national boundaries. Industrial air and water pollution, nuclear waste proliferation, increasing deforestation and soil erosion, ocean contamination, worldwide water shortages, extinction of animal and plant species, global warming, and a host of other urgent issues must be addressed internationally.

Similarly, poverty, lack of education, and poor health don't stop at any nation's borders. Whether a health worker is employed in the United States or overseas, almost every health issue he or she encounters is now a global concern. The spread of HIV and AIDS, the resurgence of tuberculosis, outbreaks of new strains of influenza, and the challenge of infant mortality are all international problems. A student dedicated to obtaining the education, training, and communication skills needed to work in these areas could make a positive contribution to the relief of human suffering.

More and more, twenty-first-century careers will require workers with skills in international communication, person-to-person interactions, languages, and cultural adaptation.

LEARN ABOUT CAREERS FOR WORKERS WITH DISABILITIES

According to the Centers for Disease Control and Prevention (CDC), about 3 percent of infants are born with a birth defect. However, the National Institute on Disability and Rehabilitation Research found that, in 2010, 11.9 percent of people in the United States had disabilities.

Many people at some time in their lives will acquire a physical, mental, or emotional disability. When planning your career, learning about careers for people with disabilities may prove to be important for your own life, or it may help a family member or friend find the information that he or she needs.

LAWS THAT OPEN UP OPPORTUNITIES FOR THOSE WITH A DISABILITY

Recently, the federal government has taken steps to end discrimination against disabled people who seek employment or who are already working. In 1990, Congress enacted the Americans

Matthew Edwards uses technology to operate his own printing company in Millersville, Maryland. Many federal, local, and private programs offer resources to disabled persons for launching their careers.

with Disabilities Act (ADA), which applies to both government and private employers. The law requires that any individual with a disability who is qualified for a specific job be given the same opportunity to be hired for that job as a person who has no disability.

The ADA also requires businesses that employ fifteen or more people to "make reasonable accommodation" to enable a qualified disabled worker to perform the job duties. For example, a deaf applicant might need a sign language interpreter for the job interview, or a worker using a wheelchair might need a ramp to be able to enter the building. The law also provides several tax advantages to help employers pay for the accommodations.

JOB ASSISTANCE PROGRAMS FOR PEOPLE WITH DISABILITIES

According to the Federal Jobs Network, well over two hundred thousand people with disabilities now work for the federal government. Government agencies also actively seek to employ qualified people with disabilities.

For persons with disabilities who plan to become entrepreneurs, the U.S. Small Business Administration (SBA) offers both information and assistance. The SBA's services include low-interest loans for those starting a business. It also offers tax forms that are easier for people with certain disabilities to use, such as forms in Braille or in recorded speech. The Job Accommodation Network provides technical assistance, consulting, and mentoring to entrepreneurs with disabilities.

FIVE WAYS YOU CAN ASSIST OTHERS WHO HAVE DISABILITIES

Even though you may not have a disability, you are likely to work side by side with others who do. The Office of Disability Employment Policy in the U.S. Department of Labor provides helpful suggestions about communicating with and assisting people with disabilities. For example:

- Treat any individual who has a disability with dignity, courtesy, and respect. Listen to him or her. Offer assistance, but do not insist or be offended if your offer is not accepted.
- Speak to the person with a disability when you approach him or her. Some people are concerned that they will say the wrong thing, so they say nothing at all.
- If you offer assistance, wait until the offer is accepted. Then listen for instructions about what the person would like you to do. Ask before you attempt to lead a person. If accepted, allow the person to hold your arm and still control his or her own movements.
- If a person uses a wheelchair, do not assume that he or she wants to be pushed. Ask first. If the person appears to be having trouble opening a door, offer assistance, but wait for his or her response.
- When speaking to a person whose hearing is impaired, gain his or her attention first. For example, tap him or her gently on the shoulder or arm. Look directly at the person and speak clearly, using short sentences.

You can find more suggestions about communicating with and assisting persons with disabilities at http://www.dol.gov/odep/pubs/fact/comucate.htm.

CAREERS FOR ALL

Many career opportunities are now available for those with physical, mental, or emotional disabilities, and more are opening up every day. Begin your career search by considering the areas that interest you most.

Some careers, of course, would not be sensible choices. However, even though a visually impaired person might not become an airline pilot, many other jobs in travel and flight would be possibilities.

If you have a disability, learn all you can about the extent of your disability and its probable course in the future. This knowledge will help you make good judgments about jobs and job training that you could pursue confidently. Consider, too, what kind of work environment would be comfortable and the kinds of accommodations a potential employer would need to provide.

Support organizations exist for almost every disability, with Web sites linking the user to sources of assistance, job training, and potential employment. Support organizations often provide information about technological advances that can enable persons with disabilities to live comfortably and work effectively. Today, a person with a disability can look forward to a valuable and satisfying career.

GLOSSARY

ACCELERATION The act or process of moving faster or happening more quickly.

ACCOMMODATION An adjustment made by an employer for the convenience or comfort of a worker with a disability.

APTITUDE An innate ability or talent.

ASSET A positive characteristic.

AUTOMATION The automatic operation of equipment.

CAREER A person's major life work.

CRITICAL THINKING The process of analyzing a situation and identifying problems.

DISABILITY An impairment or restriction in a person's ability.

DISCRIMINATION An act or policy of favoring one qualified person over another.

ECONOMY The activities related to the production and distribution of goods and services.

ENTREPRENEUR A person who organizes, operates, and assumes the financial risk involved in running a business.

GLOBALIZATION The tendency of nations, organizations, and individuals around the world to become more and more connected and interdependent.

INTERVIEW A meeting or conversation arranged to ask and answer questions. In a job interview, a potential employer assesses the qualifications of the job applicant, and the applicant finds out more about the job requirements.

JOB PROSPECT The possibility of being hired to work
in a job.

JOB SHADOWING Visiting a staff person to observe
his or her workday.

LIFESTYLE A person's habits and preferences in daily
activities, food, clothing, entertainment, and
companions.

PERVASIVENESS The state of being spread out so
thoroughly as to be seen or felt everywhere.

POTENTIAL A person's abilities or possible accomplish-
ments that have not been realized yet.

RÉSUMÉ A document describing a person's qualifications and work experience.

TECHNOLOGY The application of scientific knowledge
to accomplish practical objectives.

Job Bank
355 North River Road
Place Vanier, Tower B, 8th Floor
Mail stop VB801
Ottawa, ON K1A 0L1
Canada
(866) 789-1297
Web site: http://www.jobbank.gc.ca
Job Bank is a free citizens' service providing informa-
    tion and assistance for Canadian youth and adults in
    building careers and finding employment.

Mapping Your Future
P.O. Box 5176
Round Rock, TX 78683-5176
Web site: http://mappingyourfuture.org
Mapping Your Future is a nonprofit organization pro-
    viding career, college, financial aid, and financial
    literacy information and services for students,
    families, and schools. It offers resources on career
    selection, early awareness, and college planning.

Office of Disability Employment Policy
U.S. Department of Labor
200 Constitution Avenue NW
Washington, DC 20212
(866) 633-7365
Web site: http://www.dol.gov/odep

The mission of the Office of Disability Employment Policy is to foster, promote, and develop the welfare of disabled wage earners and job seekers and advance their opportunities for profitable employment.

U.S. Department of Education
400 Maryland Avenue SW
Washington, DC 20202
(800) 872-5327
Web site: http://www.ed.gov
The mission of the U.S. Department of Education is to promote student achievement and preparation for global competitiveness by fostering educational excellence and ensuring equal access.

WEB SITES

Due to the changing nature of Internet links, Rosen Publishing has developed an online list of Web sites related to the subject of this book. This site is updated regularly. Please use this link to access the list:

http://www.rosenlinks.com/top10/car

Christen, Carol, Richard N. Bolles, and Jean M.
Blomquist. *What Color Is Your Parachute? For Teens:
Discovering Yourself, Defining Your Future.* 2nd ed.
Berkeley, CA: Ten Speed Press, 2010.

Ferguson Publishing. *The Top 100: The Fastest-Growing
Careers for the 21st Century.* 5th ed. New York, NY:
Ferguson, 2011.

Greenland, Paul, and AnnaMarie L. Sheldon. *Career
Opportunities in Conservation and the Environment.*
New York, NY: Ferguson, 2008.

Gregory, Michael. *The Career Chronicles: An Insider's
Guide to What Jobs Are Really Like: The Good, the
Bad, and the Ugly from Over 750 Professions.*
Novato, CA: New World Library, 2008.

JIST Works, Inc., and the U.S. Department of Labor. *EZ
Occupational Outlook Handbook: Based on
Information from the U.S. Department of Labor.*
Indianapolis, IN: JIST Works, 2011.

Krasna, Heather. *Jobs That Matter: Find a Stable,
Fulfilling Career in Public Service.* Indianapolis, IN:
JIST Works, 2010.

Lore, Nicholas, and Anthony Spadafore. *Now What? The
Young Person's Guide to Choosing the Perfect
Career.* New York, NY: Simon & Schuster, 2008.

MacDougall, Debra Angel, and Elisabeth Harney
Sanders-Park. *The 6 Reasons You'll Get the Job:
What Employers Look for—Whether They Know It or
Not.* New York, NY: Prentice Hall Press, 2010.

BIBLIOGRAPHY

Association for Computing Machinery. "Computing
    Careers—Top Ten Reasons to Major in Computing."
    Retrieved October 22, 2011 (http://computing
    careers.acm.org/?page_id=4).

Burlingham, Bo, and George Gendron. "The
    Entrepreneur of the Decade." *Inc.*, April 1, 1989.
    Retrieved October 29, 2011 (http://www.inc.com/
    magazine/19890401/5602.html).

Canfield, Jack, and Janet Switzer. *The Success
    Principles: How to Get from Where You Are to Where
    You Want to Be*. New York, NY: Harper Resource
    Book, 2005.

Centers for Disease Control and Prevention. "Birth
    Defects: Data and Statistics." September 19, 2011.
    Retrieved November 12, 2011 (http://www
    .researchondisability.org/docs/default-document
    -library/annualcompendium2011.pdf).

Covey, Stephen R. *The 7 Habits of Highly Effective
    People*. New York, NY: Simon & Schuster, 1989.

FederalJobs.net. "Jobs for People with Disabilities—
    Government Jobs in the Federal Sector." 2010.
    Retrieved November 11, 2011 (http://federaljobs
    .net/disabled.htm).

Florida Department of Education. "Career and
    Education Planning Course Outline." 2006.
    Retrieved July 14, 2011 (http://www.fldoe.org/
    workforce/ced/pdf/CareerExplorationDecision
    Making.pdf).

Foundation Fighting Blindness. "Career Information for the Blind and Visually Impaired." April 2000. Retrieved November 11, 2011 (http://www.blindness.org/pdf/careerbook.pdf).

Gillis, Justin, and Celia W. Dugger. "U.N. Forecasts 10.1 Billion People by Century's End." *New York Times*, May 3, 2011. Retrieved December 31, 2011 (http://www.nytimes.com/2011/05/04/world/04population.html).

Gray, Leila. "Implantable Computers to Restore Brain Function Lost to Injury or Disease Is Keck Foundation Grant Goal." University of Washington Health Sciences, February 7, 2011. Retrieved October 22, 2011 (http://www.washington.edu/news/articles/an-implantable-computer-to-restore-brain-function-lost-to-injury-or-disease-is-goal-of-keck-foundation-grant-to-the-uw).

Greenaway, Twilight. "Your Taco, Deconstructed." *GOOD*, March 2, 2010. Retrieved November 10, 2011 (http://www.good.is/post/your-taco-deconstructed).

Groux, Catherine. "Illinois Conference Highlights Importance of College Education." *U.S. News University Connection*, August 5, 2011. Retrieved October 27, 2011 (http://www.usnewsuniversitydirectory.com/articles/illinois-conference-highlights-importance-of-colle_11676.aspx).

Henry Ford Museum. "The Life of Henry Ford." 2003.
    Retrieved October 29, 2011 (http://www.hfmgv
    .org/exhibits/hf/printdefault.asp).
Holland, John L. *Making Vocational Choices: A Theory
    of Vocational Personalities and Work Environments.*
    3rd ed. Odessa, FL: Psychological Assessment
    Resources, 1997.
Hsu, Tiffany. "College Graduates Earn 84% More Than
    High School Grads, Study Says." *Los Angeles
    Times*, August 5, 2011. Retrieved December 30,
    2011 (http://latimesblogs.latimes.com/money_
    co/2011/08/college-gradutates-pay.html).
Lohr, Steve. "More Jobs Predicted for Machines, Not
    People." *New York Times*, October 23, 2011.
    Retrieved October 25, 2011 (http://www.nytimes.
    com/2011/10/24/technology/economists
    -see-more-jobs-for-machines-not-people.html).
Maltz, Susan, and Barbara Grahn. *A Fork in the Road: A
    Career Planning Guide for Young Adults.* Manassas
    Park, VA: Impact Publications, 2003.
National Institute on Disability and Rehabilitation
    Research. "2011 Annual Disability Statistics
    Compendium." 2011. Retrieved November 12, 2011
    (http://www.researchondisability.org/docs/default-
    document-library/annualcompendium2011.pdf).
Office of Disability Employment Policy, U.S.
    Department of Labor. "Communicating with and

About People with Disabilities." Retrieved November 11, 2011 (http://www.dol.gov/odep/pubs/fact/comucate.htm).

Petrecca, Laura. "Fewer People Choose to Be Self-Employed." *USA Today*, September 9, 2011. Retrieved October 29, 2011 (http://www.usatoday.com/money/smallbusiness/2011-09-07-low-self-employment_n.htm).

Popper, Ben. "Six Personality Traits Every Small-Business Owner Should Have." BusinessInsider.com, January 14, 2011. Retrieved October 29, 2011 (http://www.entrepreneur.com/article/217837).

U.S. Bureau of Labor Statistics. "Employment Projections: Fastest-Growing Occupations." November 2009. Retrieved October 25, 2011 (http://www.bls.gov/emp/ep_table_103.htm).

U.S. Equal Opportunity Employment Commission. "Facts About the Americans with Disabilities Act." September 9, 2008. Retrieved November 12, 2011 (http://www.eeoc.gov/facts/fs-ada.html).

U.S. Small Business Administration. "People with Disabilities." Retrieved November 12, 2011 (http://www.sba.gov/content/people-with-disabilities).

Vogt, Peter. "Job Shadow for Your Career." Retrieved July 19, 2011 (http://career-advice.monster.com/job-search/career-assessment/job-shadow-for-your-career/article.aspx).

ABOUT THE AUTHOR

Molly Jones writes on health, education, careers, and contemporary issues. She is the author of seven previous books and several magazine articles and stories for children and young adults. A certified and experienced high school teacher, she has a Ph.D. in educational research with additional graduate studies in epidemiology and biostatistics. Her research has been published in *Remedial and Special Education, Journal of Early Intervention,* and *Medical Care*. She lives on Lake Murray near Columbia, South Carolina.

PHOTO CREDITS

Cover istockphoto.com/Diane Diederich; pp. 5, 10, 17, 28, 38, 50 © AP Images; p. 8 The Washington Post/Getty Images; p. 14 © Sacramento Bee/Brian Baer/ZUMA Press; p. 22 Boston Globe/Getty Images; p. 29 © Redding Record Searchlight/ZUMA Press; p. 32 © Gary Reyes/San Jose Mercury News/MCT/ZUMA Press; p. 34 moodboard/Cultura/Getty Images; p. 41 Bloomberg/Getty Images; p. 46 Boston Globe/Getty Images; interior background graphic, back cover phyZick/Shutterstock.com.

Designer: Nicole Russo; Editor: Andrea Sclarow Paskoff; Photo Researcher: Amy Feinberg